# ZOO ANIMALS
# IN THE WILD
# ALLIGATOR

## JINNY JOHNSON
## ILLUSTRATED BY GRAHAM ROSEWARNE

**W**
FRANKLIN WATTS
LONDON·SYDNEY

 An Appleseed Editions book

First published in 2006 by Franklin Watts
338 Euston Road, London NW1 3BH

Franklin Watts Australia
Hachette Children's Books
Level 17/207 Kent St, Sydney, NSW 2000

© 2006 Appleseed Editions

Created by Appleseed Editions Ltd,
Well House, Friars Hill, Guestling, East Sussex TN35 4ET

Designed by Helen James
Edited by Mary-Jane Wilkins
Illustrated by Graham Rosewarne

ISBN 0 7496 6728 1

Dewey Classification: 597.98'4

A CIP catalogue for this book is available from the British Library

Photographs by Robert E. Barber, Corbis (Theo Allofs, Tom Brakefield, John Conrad,
Tim Davis, DESPOTOVIC DUSKO / CORBIS SYGMA, Firefly Productions,
Peter Johnson, Wolfgang Kaehler, Galen Rowell, Kevin Schafer, Paul A. Souders, Roger Tidman)

Printed and bound in Thailand

# Contents

# Alligators

Alligators, with their huge tooth-lined jaws and their armour-plated skin, are fearsome creatures. They are a kind of crocodile and they have hardly changed since the days of the dinosaurs.

Alligators and crocodiles are reptiles. They are related to lizards and snakes. An alligator has a long body, a powerful tail and short stumpy legs. Much of its thick skin is covered with tough scales. The back scales contain little pieces of bone so they are extra hard and strong. They protect the alligator and make it very difficult to attack.

An alligator lies in the sun to warm up, and slips into water to cool down.

An alligator has more than 70 teeth. They are shaped for biting and holding prey, not for chewing.

# Crocodiles and alligators

How do you tell the difference between alligators and crocodiles? They are the same shape, but alligators have broader, shorter snouts than most crocodiles. Their skin is darker, too, and looks black when wet.

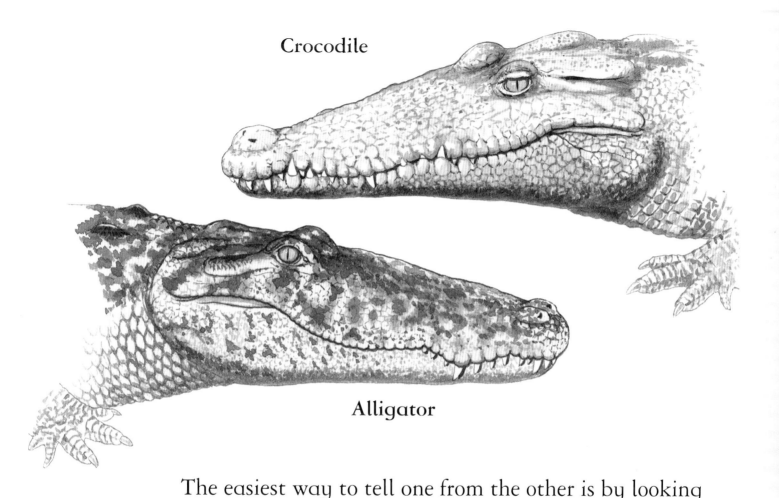

Crocodile

Alligator

The easiest way to tell one from the other is by looking at their jaws. When a crocodile's jaws are closed, the big fourth tooth on each side of the lower jaw slots into a special notch in the upper jaw. This gives the crocodile a toothy grin. An alligator's fourth tooth fits into holes in the upper jaw and can't be seen when its mouth is closed.

**An alligator spends time on land as well as in water.**

# Life in the wild

There are two kinds of alligator. American alligators live in swamps, marshes and rivers in the south-eastern United States. Chinese alligators live in a big river in China called the Yangtze.

Alligators prefer slow-moving water. They lie very still with only their eyes and nose above

The American alligator is the largest reptile in North America.

the surface, watching for prey. In winter alligators sometimes dig burrows or holes in the mud where they hide until the weather grows warmer. An alligator can even survive when the water surface freezes. It just needs to keep its nose clear of the ice so it can breathe.

An alligator is almost invisible as it lies in the water.

A Chinese alligator is half the size of an American alligator.

There are plenty of American and Chinese alligators living in zoos, although Chinese alligators are becoming rare in the wild.

# Life in the zoo

Zoo alligators need water, warmth and somewhere to lie on land, just as wild alligators do.

Although alligators spend much of their time in water,
they must have some land where they can lie in the sun.

In warm, subtropical areas zoo alligators can live in outdoor enclosures all year round. Further north, alligators need to live indoors in heated homes – at least during the winter months. Many zoos provide heat lamps for alligators to warm themselves under and shady areas where they can cool down.

It's fun to watch alligators – knowing that you are safely out of their reach!

# On the move

Alligators are expert swimmers and more at home in water than on land. But they can run surprisingly fast for short distances on their strong plump legs.

Alligators move more awkwardly on land than in water and tire quickly.

An alligator can walk underwater on the bottom of a river or enclosure.

In water an alligator holds its legs against its body and swims by moving its long body and pushing with its broad, heavy tail. Alligators have webbed back feet with flaps of skin between their toes. When they float they hold out their feet to steady themselves in the water.

Webbing between the toes makes an alligator's feet into useful paddles.

# An alligator's day

Alligators, like other reptiles, cannot keep themselves warm. Instead, they rely on the sun for warmth.

An alligator warming itself in the sun.

An alligator slips
quietly into the water.

Every morning they stretch out in the sun
on a marsh bank or rocks. When they've
warmed up enough they slip into the water
to keep cool, then sunbathe again in the
late afternoon.

Alligators usually hunt at night. But if
something comes close enough during the
day they are always ready to strike.

Zoo alligators don't
have to hunt for
their food so they
spend much of their
day lying in the sun
or under heat lamps.
Sometimes zoo
keepers give them
some fish to catch.

# Feeding time

Alligators are predators – they live by killing and eating other creatures. They'll eat anything they can catch from birds, snakes and turtles to animals as big as deer and cows.

An alligator lies like a floating log in the water and keeps watch for prey. If an animal comes close to the water's edge to drink, the alligator lunges forward with amazing speed to seize it. It drowns its prey before tearing it to pieces with its teeth.

An alligator's jaws are strong enough to crush a hard-shelled creature such as a turtle.

Zoo alligators eat meat, just like wild alligators. Their keepers feed them creatures such as rats, as well as some beef, chicken and rabbit.

Alligators also eat carrion – animals that are already dead.

In summer alligators eat lots of food and build up plenty of fat on their bodies. When the weather grows cool they eat much less. They can go without food for weeks in winter.

Alligators cannot chew so they have to swallow their prey whole or in big chunks.

# Eyes, ears and nose

As alligators lie in wait for prey
their eyes, ears and nose are always
alert for any sign of possible food.

A transparent
third eyelid
covers and
protects an
alligator's
eyes when
under water.

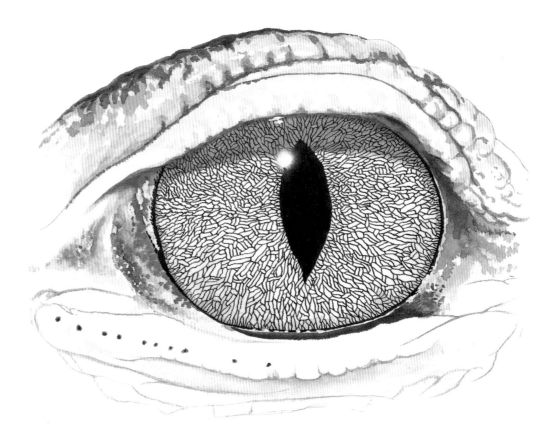

Alligators have good eyesight and they can see well at night, when they do most of their hunting. Alligators hear well, too, and their ears are protected by small flaps when underwater. The nostrils, which are at the tip of the nose, also close up in water.

An alligator's senses are perfectly adapted for life in water.

# Laying eggs

Most reptiles do very little for their young, but alligators are caring parents.

An alligator's nest mound measures between 1 and 2 metres across and can be a metre high.

Female alligators make nests in the zoo, just as they do in the wild. But the zoo might take away most of the eggs as they don't have space for 45 new baby alligators every year!

An alligator mother places her eggs gently in her nest.

When she is ready to lay her eggs a female alligator makes a nest. She scrapes together a mound of plants and earth with her feet on the river bank or at the edge of a swamp or marsh.

She makes a hollow in the mound and lays about 45 eggs, which she then covers with plants. As the plants rot, they heat the mound and keep the eggs warm. The mother stays close by to guard the nest.

# Time to hatch

After about 65 days the baby alligators are ready to hatch and start making high-pitched peeping sounds from inside their eggs. When their mother hears her young calling, she comes to dig the eggs out of the mound.

She may help to crack open the eggs, too. The newly hatched babies are tiny compared with their mother – only about 23 centimetres long – that's about as long as this page.

A young alligator struggles out of its egg.

A mother alligator carefully carries her young to water. She then gently shakes her head to encourage her babies to swim out of her mouth.

The alligators' mother gathers up the babies in her mouth, seven or eight at a time. She carries them to a safe area of water.

Once in the water young alligators gather in groups called pods.

# Young alligators

A mother alligator keeps a close eye on her little ones. If they stray too far they may be snapped up by hungry birds and large fish.

The baby alligators swim as soon as they reach water and they start feeding on small prey such as insects, snails and fish. They are about three times their hatching size by the end of their first year and keep growing until they are about eight years old.

Baby alligators have yellow or cream markings that fade as they grow.

Alligators live for about 35 to 50 years in the wild, but in zoos some live to be 70 or more.

Growth slows down at eight, but alligators don't stop growing altogether until they are about 25 years old.

Alligators must find their own food from the moment they hatch.

# Keeping in touch

Alligators are some of the noisiest of all reptiles. Babies call to their mother before they are even out of the egg and mothers and young grunt to one another to keep in touch.

Baby alligators call to their mother if they are in danger.

Male alligators make loud bellowing calls that sound a bit like a lion's roar. Their roars can be heard from quite a distance, as well as under water.

Alligators also attract attention by slapping their jaws down on to the water surface, making a loud noise and lots of bubbles. A male may do this to show other alligators that this is his area and he is in charge.

**Alligators are noisier than ever during the breeding season when they are looking for mates.**

# Alligator fact file

Here is some more information about alligators.
Your mum or dad might like to read this, or
you could read these pages together.

An alligator is a reptile and belongs to the crocodile group.
There are two kinds – the American alligator and the Chinese
alligator. There are also some close relatives of alligators
called caimans, which live in Central and South America.

## Where alligators live

The American alligator lives in the south-eastern USA.
The Chinese alligator lives in some parts of the Yangtze River in China.

## Alligator numbers

Fifty years ago the American alligator was becoming very rare because
so many were hunted and killed for their skin. Experts were worried that
alligators would disappear for ever and they were given official protection.
Numbers increased very quickly and there are now plenty of American
alligators. Chinese alligators are rare in the wild – there may be only 200
left – but there are some living in protected reserves and in zoos.

## Size

A full-grown male American alligator is about 5 metres long and can weigh 250 kilograms, although most are smaller. Females grow up to 2.7 metres long. Chinese alligators are only 2 metres long and weigh about 40 kilograms.

## Find out more

Check out these websites

Smithsonian National Zoo
http://nationalzoo.si.edu/Animals/ReptilesAmphibians/Facts/FactSheets/Americanalligator.cfm

National Parks Conservation Association
http://www.npca.org/marine_and_coastal/marine_wildlife/alligator.asp

Chinese alligator
http://www.flmnh.ufl.edu/natsci/herpetology/brittoncrocs/csp_asin.htm

Oakland Zoo
http://www.oaklandzoo.org/atoz/azaligtr.html

# Words to remember

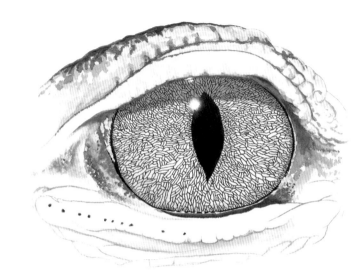

**breeding season**
The time when alligators find
a mate and lay eggs.

**dinosaur**
A kind of reptile that lived on
Earth thousands of years ago.

**enclosure**
The area where an animal lives in a zoo.

**mate**
Male and female alligators pair up to lay eggs.
An alligator's partner is called its mate.

**predator**
An animal that lives by hunting and killing other animals.

**prey**
An animal that is hunted and eaten by another animal.

**reptile**
A cold-blooded animal that has a backbone.

**scales**
Hard pieces of skin that cover a reptile's body.

**subtropical**
Parts of the world where the weather is never really cold.

**swamp**
An area of ground that is always wet and sometimes covered with water.

**transparent**
Something that is clear and can be seen through.

**webbed feet**
Webbed feet have flaps of skin between the toes. This makes the feet into paddles to help the alligator move in water.

# Index